The Old Testament in Living Pictures

A Photo Guide to the Old Testament

BY DAVID S. ALEXANDER

G/L REGAL BOOKS

A Division of G/L Publications
Glendale, California, U.S.A.

Published in North America by
Regal Books Division, G/L Publications
Glendale, California 91209, U.S.A.

Copyright © 1973 Lion Publishing

Photographs and notes by
David S. Alexander

Scripture quotations from The Living Bible,
reproduced by permission of Kenneth Taylor.

ISBN 0-8307-0225-3
Library of Congress Catalog Card No applied for.

First edition 1973

Printed in Great Britain by
Purnell and Sons Ltd, Paulton, U.K.

Introduction

It is a rewarding experience to be able to visit the Middle East, and see for oneself the places where the events of the Bible took place. But many of the Old Testament sites are not on the main tourist routes — and in any case not many will have the good fortune to be able to make such a trip at all.

This book will help fill the need. The pictures recapture the way of life and events so graphically described in the Old Testament. They open a window on the history, literature and environment of Bible times. They show the relevance of some of the archaeological discoveries made over the last century which bring us face to face with the ancient civilizations flourishing in Bible times.

The Old Testament spans the ages, from the beginning of time to the dark days after the fall of Jerusalem, the exile of God's people to Babylon and their return. The narrative ranges from history to poetry, from law to prophecy. Written over more than a thousand years, it both reflects the age in which it was written and carries a power which makes it relevant to all time.

The fact that the Old Testament so often reflects contemporary life means that our understanding of it can be helped as we see it against its background. The life of the desert tent-dwellers enables us to picture Abraham and the patriarchs. The cracked, sun-bleached salt rocks near the Dead Sea evoke the catastrophe which overwhelmed Sodom and Gomorrah. The mountains of Sinai and barren wastes of the Negev desert vividly reflect the setting of the wanderings in the wilderness and giving of the law.

Some of the sites have an interest which is more directly historical. Today there may be no more than a litter of ruins and fallen stones: but these are the actual remains of Shiloh or Shechem, Lachish or Gezer. Some of the archaeological sites are easier to imagine as they appeared in Bible times: Jericho, or Megiddo, with its Canaanite 'high place' and buildings from the time of Solomon, or Hazor with its gateway and pillars—and even a wall hastily built because of impending invasion. The Old Testament is not a collection of myths. It was about real people living in real places whose remains can still be seen today. The narrative has, in fact, at many places been shown to be reliable and relevant by modern discoveries. The historical accuracy of the Bible has been rediscovered too by many who read it in the light of contemporary research.

A shepherd leading his flock, gazelles on the mountains, wool being dyed scarlet, water in the desert, the cedars of Lebanon . . . much of the familiar language of the Old Testament lives afresh when it is pictured in this way. Today it is only in traditional areas that one can still see the wooden plough, the camel market, the flocks round a well, so it is good that as city life and mechanization increase the traditional setting of biblical life can be recorded and appreciated while it is still possible.

The main aim of this book is to encourage the reader to turn again to the whole Bible for himself. There he will see God in action with real people in actual situations. God who called out a people to live in faith in himself, who delivered them from slavery and showed them the way to live, is the same God as the God and Father of Jesus Christ, who showed the way to newness of life and won man's freedom by his death and resurrection. It is this faith, the theme of this book, which is so vital and relevant today.

Donald J. Wiseman
*Professor of Assyriology in the
University of London*

Contents

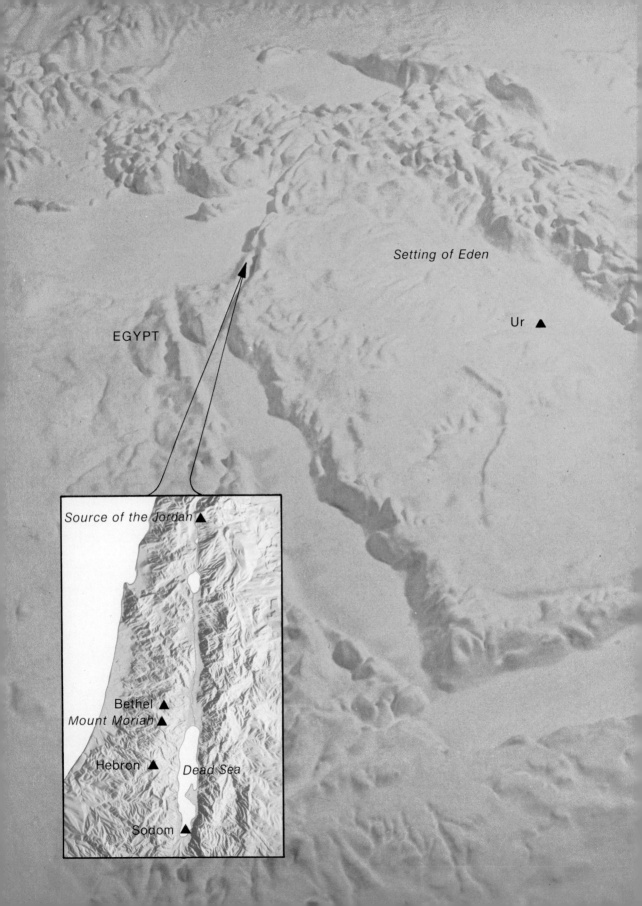

Setting of Eden

Ur ▲

EGYPT

Source of the Jordan ▲

Bethel ▲
Mount Moriah ▲

Hebron ▲

Dead Sea

Sodom ▲

PART ONE

Fathers of a Nation

Creation

"When God began creating the heavens and the earth . . ."   Genesis 1:1

Ancient Israel extended 'from Dan to Beersheba'. Near Dan in the extreme north is the source of the River Jordan. The water is forced through the stones with an energy and power that makes it immediately a rushing stream. Genesis 1 proclaims God as source and maker of all things. The teeming universe sprang from his command with all the energy and life of a mountain stream. Presented as a drama in six acts, God's creativity culminated in the creation of man. And on the seventh day he rested.

Eden

"The time came when the Lord God formed a man's body from the dust of the ground and breathed into it the breath of life. And man became a living person. Then the Lord God planted a garden in Eden, to the east, and placed in the garden the man he had formed. The Lord God planted all sorts of beautiful trees there in the garden, trees producing the choicest of fruit. At the center of the garden he placed the Tree of Life, and also the Tree of Conscience, giving knowledge of Good and Bad."   Genesis 2:7-9

The picture was taken further down the Jordan River, south of the Lake of Galilee. Eden itself was given a setting 'in the east', the rivers watering it evoking the richness of the Mesopotamian basin before man made it a desert. For man chose independence of God rather than dependence on him. He disobeyed him to win freedom, but lost the freedom of being the man he was made to be. Inevitably, fellowship with God was broken; cut off from God, the source of life, man and all creation was turned from good to evil.

14

The call of Abraham

"God told Abram, 'Leave your own country behind you, and your own people, and go to the land I will guide you to. If you do, I will cause you to become the father of a great nation; I will bless you and make your name famous, and you will be a blessing to many others . . .' So Abram departed as the Lord had instructed him . . . He took his wife Sarai, his nephew Lot, and all his wealth . . . and finally arrived in Canaan."
Genesis 12:1-5

God's way of making a new start was by calling one man. From him was to come a great people. Abraham left a brilliant civilization, Ur of the Chaldees, for a nomad life, in obedience to God's call. The bedouin sheikh pictured here shows how the desert 'dwellers in tents' have lived for centuries. Using goats' skins in winter and sack-cloth in the heat of summer, their tents are spread with carpets. The men recline on cushions round the earth fire-place. A more settled way of life would not enable them to find the best grazing for their livestock, their means of livelihood. So closely interdependent were animals and men in the nomad encampment that it was said of Abraham, 'he had sheep, oxen, he-asses, menservants, maid-servants, she-asses, and camels.'

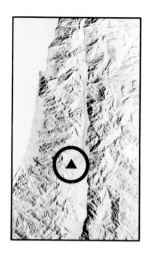

Abraham and Lot

"Then Abram talked it over with Lot. 'This fighting between our men has got to stop,' he said. 'We can't afford to let a rift develop between our clans. Close relatives such as we are must present a united front! I'll tell you what we'll do. Take your choice of any section of the land you want, and we will separate. If you want that part over there to the east, then I'll stay here in the western section. Or, if you want the west, then I'll go over there to the east.' Lot took a long look at the fertile plains of the Jordan River, well watered everywhere . . . So that is what Lot chose — the Jordan valley to the east of them. He went there with his flocks and servants, and thus he and Abram parted company. For Abram stayed in the land of Canaan, while Lot lived among the cities of the plain, settling at a place near the city of Sodom. The men of this area were unusually wicked, and sinned greatly against Jehovah."
Genesis 13:8-13

Famine had driven Abraham and his family to Egypt. On his return to Canaan after the long, weary trek up through the Negev desert, he was rich in flocks and herds and tents, but the herdsmen were quarrelling bitterly. The only way was to separate. Abraham would rather have the hard life and poor grazing on the mountains of Judea than the richness of the valley if it was only to cause bitterness and family feud. It also says something for Abraham's attitude that he allowed his younger nephew first choice. Lot's decision, as it turned out, was a moral one. The rich cities of the plain had the tempting night-life. Lot journeyed east.

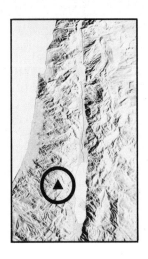

Hebron

"After Lot was gone, the Lord said to Abram, 'Look as far as you can see in every direction, for I am going to give it all to you and your descendants. And I am going to give you so many descendants that, like dust, they can't be counted! Hike in all directions and explore the new possessions I am giving you.' Then Abram moved his tent to the oaks of Mamre, near Hebron, and built an altar to Jehovah there."
Genesis 13:14-18

Hebron stands at a height of over 3,000 feet in the mountains south of Jerusalem. The Arabic name for Abraham is al-Khalil er-Rahman, the Friend of the Lord, hence the Arabic name for Hebron—Khalil. Abraham bought a plot of ground with a cave here, as a family burying-ground. He bought it from Hittites who were settled in the area, and the details of the negotiations recorded in Genesis 23 reflect the intricacies of Hittite laws and customs of the time. The burial-place. the Cave of Machpelah, is now a shrine. The building over it, pictured here, goes back to the time of Herod, with additions in Byzantine and Crusader times. Mamre, where Abraham lived, is a mile or two south of Hebron.

Mount Moriah

"Later on, God tested Abraham's faith and obedience. 'Abraham!' God called. 'Yes, Lord?' he replied. 'Take with you your only son—yes, Isaac whom you love so much—and go to the land of Moriah and sacrifice him there as a burnt offering upon one of the mountains which I'll point out to you!' The next morning Abraham got up early, chopped wood for a fire upon the altar, saddled his donkey, and took with him his son Isaac and two young men who were his servants, and started off to the place where God had told him to go. On the third day of the journey Abraham saw the place in the distance. 'Stay here with the donkey,' Abraham told the young men, 'and the lad and I will travel yonder and worship, and then come right back.' "
Genesis 22:1-5

At Mamre God had told Sarah she would have a child—and she had laughed in sheer disbelief, for she was past the age for child-bearing. Yet God had promised that Abraham's descendants would be like the stars in number, and like the sand on the sea-shore. The child Isaac was God's fulfilment of his own promise. So when God then seemed to be calling Abraham to the mountains of Moriah to sacrifice his son, the realization of God's own promise, it was a supreme test of Abraham's trust in God's promises as well as his natural love for his son. Abraham's faith was vindicated: a ram caught in a thicket was provided for the sacrifice instead of Isaac. The mountains of Moriah were also to be the site of Solomon's Temple (2 Chronicles 3: 1): the rocky top of the temple hill is enshrined in the Mosque of Omar which stands there now.

The Dead Sea

" 'What relatives do you have here in the city?' the men asked. 'Get them out of this place—sons-in-law, sons, daughters, or anyone else. For we will destroy the city completely. The stench of the place has reached to heaven and God has sent us to destroy it.' So Lot rushed out to tell his daughters' fiancés, 'Quick, get out of the city, for the Lord is going to destroy it.' But the young men looked at him as though he had lost his senses."
Genesis 19:12-14

The site of the cities of Sodom and Gomorrah is thought to be now covered by the waters of the south end of the Dead Sea. Certainly the acrid reek in the air and the rocks bare of vegetation evoke the catastrophe which overwhelmed the cities whose corruption made them fit only for destruction. The Dead Sea, or Salt Sea, lies at the deepest point in the long rift valley down which flows the River Jordan. As the heat of the sun evaporates the water, the concentrates of potash and other chemicals build up to amount to 25 per cent of the water content:

Pillars of salt

"Then the Lord rained down fire and flaming tar from heaven upon Sodom and Gomorrah, and utterly destroyed them, along with the other cities and villages of the plain, eliminating all life—people, plants, and animals alike. But Lot's wife looked back as she was following along behind him, and became a pillar of salt." Genesis 19:24-26

Lot escaped alive only because of Abraham's pleading before God. His wife, hankering for the old life, was overwhelmed like the victims of Vesuvius at Pompeii. The great pillars of salt at the south end of the lake bear silent witness both to God's judgement in destruction and to his mercy in answering Abraham's prayer.

A wife for Isaac

"The servant took with him ten of Abraham's camels loaded with samples of the best of everything his master owned, and journeyed to Iraq, to Nahor's village. There he made the camels kneel down outside the town, beside a spring. It was evening, and the women of the village were coming to draw water. 'O Jehovah, the God of my master,' he prayed, 'show kindness to my master Abraham and help me to accomplish the purpose of my journey. See, here I am, standing beside this spring, and the girls of the village are coming out to draw water. This is my request: When I ask one of them for a drink and she says, "Yes, certainly, and I will water your camels too!" — let her be the one you have appointed as Isaac's wife. That is how I will know.' As he was still speaking to the Lord about this, a beautiful young girl named Rebekah arrived with a water jug on her shoulder and filled it at the spring."
Genesis 24:10-16

Abraham sent his chief steward to his own home-country to seek a wife for his son Isaac. The steward's prayer was answered: Rebekah was the daughter of Abraham's nephew, and, as it turned out, a wife whom Isaac truly loved.

Bethel

"So Jacob left Beer-sheba and journeyed toward Haran. That night, when he stopped to camp at sundown, he found a rock for a headrest and lay down to sleep, and dreamed that a staircase reached from earth to heaven, and he saw the angels of God going up and down upon it. At the top of the stairs stood the Lord. 'I am Jehovah,' he said, 'the God of Abraham, and of your father Isaac. The ground you are lying on is yours! I will give it to you and to your descendants. For you will have descendants as many as dust. . . .' The next morning he got up very early and set his stone headrest upright as a memorial pillar, and poured olive oil over it. He named the place Bethel."
Genesis 28:10-14, 18, 19

'Bethel' means 'House of God'. At first sight it hardly seemed that to a lonely, miserable young man leaving home. It was an area of steep, stony, forbidding hills and valleys. But in his dream the stony hill became a staircase filled with the messengers of God. In the morning the rock which was his pillow was set up as an altar to God. For there God renewed the promise made to Jacob's father. Bethel was later to play a major role in Israel's history: the resting-place of the ark, a sanctuary visited by Samuel and later adopted by Jeroboam as a sanctuary for the northern kingdom to rival Jerusalem.

Grain in Egypt

"When Jacob heard that there was grain available in Egypt he said to his sons, 'Why are you standing around looking at one another? I have heard that there is grain available in Egypt. Go down and buy some for us before we all starve to death.' So Joseph's ten older brothers went down to Egypt to buy grain. However, Jacob wouldn't let Joseph's younger brother Benjamin go with them, for fear some harm might happen to him . . . So it was that Israel's sons arrived in Egypt along with many others from many lands to buy food, for the famine was severe in Canaan as it was everywhere else. Since Joseph was governor of all Egypt, and in charge of the sale of the grain, it was to him that his brothers came . . ."
Genesis 42:1-6

A rural economy was a precarious one: lack of rain and a poor harvest soon caused hardship and famine. Refugees from famine would pour into the areas known to be better off. Joseph, the insufferable younger brother sold into slavery years before, now had power of life and death over the brothers who had wronged him. For Joseph had had the forethought and administrative skill to store grain from the good years in preparation for the bad. From being a slave he became second only to Pharaoh. But the good fortune of the children of Israel in Egypt was not to last. After Joseph's death they were increasingly enslaved, burdened under their task-masters, crying out for deliverance.

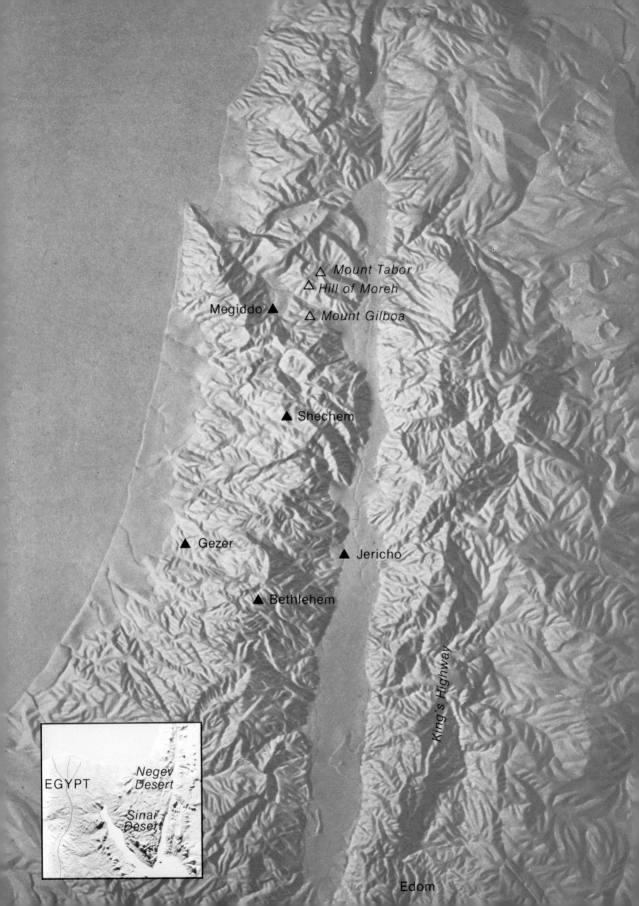

Mount Tabor
Hill of Moreh

Megiddo
Mount Gilboa

Shechem

Gezer

Jericho

Bethlehem

King's Highway

EGYPT
Negev Desert
Sinai Desert

Edom

PART TWO

Freedom and a New Life

The call of Moses

"One day as Moses was tending the flock of his father-in-law Jethro, the priest of Midian, out at the edge of the desert near Horeb, the mountain of God, suddenly the Angel of Jehovah appeared to him as a flame of fire in a bush. When Moses saw that the bush was on fire and that it didn't burn up, he went over to investigate. Then God called out to him, 'Moses! Moses!' 'Who is it?' Moses asked . . ."
Exodus 3:1-4

Moses was far from the court of Pharaoh, the place of his upbringing. Taking the law into his own hands, he had struck a blow for his people's freedom — but the only result was his own retreat to the desert of Sinai. It was there, many years later, that God revealed himself to Moses: the God of his fathers, the God whose name was 'I AM WHO I AM', the God who would not only deliver his people but would call and equip Moses to be the instrument of deliverance.

A plague of locusts

"So Moses lifted his rod and Jehovah caused an east wind to blow all that day and night; and when it was morning, the east wind had brought the locusts. And the locusts covered the land of Egypt from border to border; it was the worst locust plague in all Egyptian history; and there will never again be another like it. For the locusts covered the face of the earth and blotted out the sun so that the land was darkened; and they ate every bit of vegetation . . . there remained not one green thing . . ."
Exodus 10:13-15

Pharaoh would not let the people of Israel go. One plague followed another. Pharaoh realized only too well that he was fighting God himself. But he only hardened his heart still further. And the great natural catastrophes went on, one inexorably leading onto the next: an abnormally high Nile, bringing down red earth and deadly bacteria, would kill the fish. Frogs left the polluted river to plague the land, and from their rotting carcases came plagues of mosquitoes, flies and the cattle pest on the cattle in the fields. So it went on: the locusts were blown in on the wind to devastate the land afresh. Pharaoh—a god to his people because of his apparent control over the regular seasons of the Nile—was no match for the Lord of heaven and earth.

The wilderness

"The people growled and complained to Moses. 'Give us water!' they wailed . . . Then Moses pleaded with Jehovah."
Exodus 17:2-4

The Sinai peninsula is mountainous, rocky desert. Temperatures soar under the hot sun. The glorious deliverance from Egypt was soon forgotten as the people faced the harsh realities of lack of water and food. But God showed that he would sustain those he saved: he showed Moses the water-bearing rock at Horeb. He sent quails, flocks of migrating birds easy to catch for food. He sent manna, a small, white, honey-tasting substance. Tempted in the wilderness, Jesus took on his lips the key phrases of the experience of Israel: including the fact that man does not live by bread alone, but by every word that comes from the mouth of God.

Sinai

"On the morning of the third day there was a terrific thunder and lightning storm, and a huge cloud came down upon the mountain, and there was a long, loud blast as from a ram's horn; and all the people trembled. Moses led them out from the camp to meet God, and they stood at the foot of the mountain . . ."
Exodus 19:16, 17

God did not leave his people to wander without guidance and direction. His presence went with them by night and day. He also gave them, in the Ten Commandments and in the law generally, instructions on how to live. And in doing so he laid down a pattern of morality of universal significance.
The God of holiness was also a God of love, infinitely concerned for the welfare of his people.

41

Sanctuary in the wilderness

"Jehovah said to Moses, '. . . I want the people of Israel to make me a sacred Temple where I can live among them. This home of mine shall be a tent pavilion—a Tabernacle. I will give you a drawing of the construction plan, and the details of each furnishing. Using acacia wood, make an Ark 3¾ feet long, 2¼ feet wide, and 2¼ feet high. Overlay it inside and outside with pure gold . . . Then make a table of acacia wood . . . Make a lampstand of pure, beaten gold . . .'"
Exodus 25:1, 8-11, 23, 31

The tabernacle, or tent, which was to be God's sanctuary in the wilderness, was modelled on other portable sanctuaries known to us from Egyptian illustrations. Many of the details symbolized the relationship of God to his people. They were also practical. The acacia tree, for instance, was one of the very few available in the desert—as is still the case today in the Negev desert and Sinai peninsula. The gold would have been beaten from the plunder taken out of Egypt; silver, jewellery, linen and other materials also brought from Egypt; the main goat-hair covering made from the skins of their flocks.

A pagan altar

"The Lord then told Moses to tell the people of Israel, 'I am Jehovah your God, so don't act like heathen — like the people of Egypt where you lived so long, or the people of Canaan where I am going to take you . . . Anyone — whether an Israelite or a foreigner living among you — who sacrifices his child as a burnt offering to Molech shall without fail be stoned by his peers. And I myself will turn against that man and cut him off from all his people, because he has given his child to Molech, thus making my Tabernacle unfit for me to live in, and insulting my holy name.'"
Leviticus 18:1-3; 20:2-3

The law was given not only for Israel's present but also for the future. And it prepared the people not only for a new life in the promised land but for a fight for survival. The picture here is of an altar to the god Moloch, or Molech, at Byblos, Lebanon. The stone enclosure was for child-sacrifice. Nearby stand receptacles for the blood and for the rest of the disgusting pagan ritual. God's concern to keep his people from moral pollution was no mere sentiment. Physical death was preferable to the corruption of his people and the end of his whole plan of salvation for them and for the world. The destruction of the Canaanites was not out of concern for racial purity but a matter of judgement on utter corruption. The Amorites had been given 400 years to mend their ways (Genesis 15: 16).

A law of love

*"You must not steal nor lie nor defraud.
You must not swear to a falsehood, thus
bringing a reproach upon the name
of your God, for I am Jehovah. You shall
not rob nor oppress anyone, and you
shall pay your hired workers promptly.
If something is due them, don't even
keep it overnight. You must not curse
the deaf nor trip up a blind man as he
walks. Fear your God; I am Jehovah!
Judges must always be just in their
sentences, not noticing whether a person
is poor or rich; they must always be
perfectly fair. Don't gossip. Don't falsely
accuse your neighbor of some crime,
for I am Jehovah."*
Leviticus 19:11-16

The law was moral, ceremonial and social.
Detailed laws of food and hygiene
reflect the climate and other local
conditions in their concern for the
people's health. Laws were designed to
promote social justice, to safeguard the
weak against exploitation by the rich, to
protect those who could not protect
themselves. Laws for the use of the land
were designed for its conservation and
highest productivity. The local applications
may not be relevant in other countries
and at other times, but the basic concern
must be the same: loving the Lord our
God must result in loving our neighbour
as ourselves.

A law for every home

"O Israel, listen: Jehovah is our God, Jehovah alone. You must love him with all your heart, soul, and might. And you must think constantly about these commandments I am giving you today . . . write them on the doorposts of your house!"
Deuteronomy 6:4-6, 9

In literal obedience to the command, Jewish households have trȧditionally put this passage and the similar one in Deuteronomy 11: 13-21 in a box attached to the door-post. Called a 'Mezuzah', it seems that it was introduced by the Hasidim Jews in the second century BC in order to counter the increasing influence of Hellenistic Greek culture.

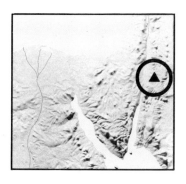

The King's Highway

"While Moses was at Kadesh he sent messengers to the king of Edom: '. . . Please let us pass through your country. We will be careful not to go through your planted fields, nor through your vineyards; we won't even drink water from your wells, but will stay on the main road and not leave it until we have crossed your border on the other side.'"
Numbers 20:14, 17

The picture shows the view the messengers would have had, looking across to the mountains of Edom. Moses' plan was to strike across to the main north-south highway which ran through Edomite territory: but Edom would not have it. The frustration and constant delay and further wandering in the desert must have seemed interminable.

Jericho

"At dawn of the seventh day they started out again, but this time they went around the city not once, but seven times. The seventh time, as the priests blew a long, loud trumpet blast, Joshua yelled to the people, 'Shout! The Lord has given us the city!'"
Joshua 6:15, 16

The forty years of wandering in the desert were over. But the entry into the promised land was not to be an easy end to all the people's problems. Jericho was only the first of the cities that had to be taken. It owed its position to its water-supply — the well that featured later in the story of Elisha. The mound of ancient Jericho, topped by the white hut, has remains going back to long before Joshua's time: it had already been destroyed and rebuilt several times, and as it was allowed to remain in ruins for centuries after Israel's attack it was unlikely to provide direct evidence of this actual incident. However, much that has been found there gives a commentary on many centuries of Old Testament history.

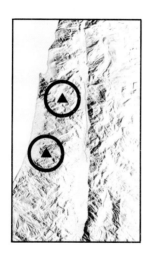

Gezer

"During the attack on Lachish, King Horam of Gezer arrived with his army to try to help defend the city, but Joshua's men killed him and destroyed his entire army. The Israeli army then captured Eglon on the first day and, as at Lachish, they killed everyone in the city."
Joshua 10:33-35

After attacking the cities near Jericho, Joshua cut across to the key fortified cities in the foothills of the mountains guarding the main highway on the plain: Lachish (see page 104) and Gezer. Among extensive ruins from this time is a complex water tunnel. Other ruins remain from the time of Solomon, who rebuilt the city. Among the objects discovered was the Gezer Calendar, a simple aid for remembering the agricultural seasons (now in the Istanbul Archaeological Museum).

Megiddo

"Here is a list of the kings destroyed by Joshua and the armies of Israel on the west side of the Jordan . . . The king of Jericho . . . The king of Megiddo . . . in all, thirty-one kings."
Joshua 12:7, 9, 21, 24

At the major archaeological site of Megiddo (see too pages 93 and 100), in one of the lowest layers uncovered, is this Canaanite altar or 'high place'. Called high places because they were originally sited on hill-tops, these pagan sanctuaries were later frequently condemned by the prophets of Israel.

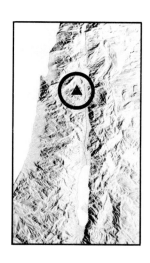

Mount Tabor

"Then Deborah said to Barak, 'Now is the time for action! The Lord leads on! He has already delivered Sisera into your hand!' So Barak led his ten thousand men down the slopes of Mount Tabor into battle. Then the Lord threw the enemy into a panic, both the soldiers and the charioteers, and Sisera leaped from his chariot and escaped on foot."
Judges 4:14, 15

In the period of the Judges a pattern recurs: the people turn away from God; they suffer judgement in the form of invasion or enemy occupation; they cry to God for help; he raises up a deliverer to free them. The 1850-foot Mount Tabor in Galilee, with its commanding views and distinctive rounded shape, was the scene of this confrontation with the Canaanite general Sisera. Deborah's magnificent song of triumph tells what happened. It seems that a sudden cloudburst turned the Kishon brook into a raging torrent, which swept many of Sisera's chariots away. The rest, clogged in the mud, would have been an easy prey.

Gideon

"Gideon and his army got an early start and went as far as the spring of Harod. The armies of Midian were camped north of them, down in the valley beside the hill of Moreh . . ." Judges 7:1

So the drama of Gideon's attack on the hosts of the Midianites unfolds. Down in the valley below the slopes of Gilboa the pools from the waters of the spring Harod reflect the sky. There Gideon reduced his army to a small, crack fighting-force. The hill of Moreh opposite marks the place in the valley where the army of Midian was camped — and where Gideon led his surprise attack.

Shechem

"Then the citizens of Shechem and Beth-millo called a meeting under the oak beside the garrison at Shechem, and Abimelech was acclaimed king of Israel. When Jotham heard about this, he stood at the top of Mount Gerizim and shouted across to the men of Shechem, 'If you want God's blessing, listen to me! Once upon a time the trees decided to elect a king . . .'"
Judges 9:6-8

At Shechem Abraham camped by 'the oak of Moreh'. Here Jacob buried the 'strange gods', and Joseph sought his brothers. It was the central place where Joshua gathered the elders, just before his death. But in the time of the Judges, Shechem was still a centre of Canaanite worship. A temple to Baal was destroyed in this story, after Jotham had used his parable to attempt to turn the people from Abimelech. Later in Israel's history Jeroboam I made the town his capital for a time, and after the exile it became the chief city of the Samaritans. Excavations have revealed buildings going back to Canaanite times, including this wall and gateway.

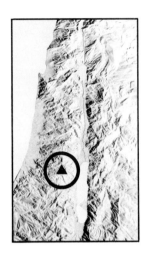

Bethlehem

"One day Naomi said to Ruth, 'My dear, isn't it time that I try to find a husband for you, and get you happily married again? The man I'm thinking of is Boaz! He has been so kind to us and is a close relative. I happen to know that he will be winnowing barley tonight out on the threshing-floor. Now do what I tell you — bathe and put on some perfume and some nice clothes and go on down to the threshing-floor . . .'"
Ruth 3:1-3

Bethlehem, 'house of bread', straddles a ridge high in the hills of Judea.
Naomi, with her husband and family, had had to flee from Bethlehem to Moab to escape famine. There her husband died, as did her son who married 'Ruth the Moabitess'. With a lyrical simplicity and restraint the story tells how their kinsman honoured his responsibilities towards Ruth — and only at the end do we discover that these were the ancestors of King David himself, and hence the forebears of Jesus who was born in Bethlehem, City of David. The story is set in the period of the Judges, and in its simple beauty shows something of the rural background to a time which was otherwise such a succession of upheavals and wars.

Tyre ▲

▲ Hazor

Mount Carmel △

Megiddo ▲   ▲ Jezreel

△ *Mount Gilboa*

SAMARIA

▲ Shiloh

Gezer ▲

▲ Gibeah
Kiriath-jearim ▲   ▲ **Jerusalem**

Lachish ▲

▲ Hebron

▲ Ein Gedi

PART THREE

A Nation under God

Shiloh

"Little Samuel was helping the Lord by assisting Eli. Messages from the Lord were very rare in those days, but one night after Eli had gone to bed (he was almost blind with age by now), and Samuel was sleeping in the Temple near the Ark, the Lord called out, 'Samuel! Samuel!' 'Yes?' Samuel replied. 'What is it?' . . . As Samuel grew, the Lord was with him and people listened carefully to his advice. And all Israel from Dan to Beer-sheba knew that Samuel was going to be a prophet of the Lord. Then the Lord began to give messages to him there at the Tabernacle in Shiloh, and he passed them on to the people of Israel."
1 Samuel 3:1-4, 19-21

Shiloh now is no more than a ruin of stones on a hill in Samaria. At the time of the Judges it was the principal sanctuary of the Israelites. By Eli's time the tent, or tabernacle, had become some kind of temple. Here Hannah, childless and 'deeply distressed . . . prayed to the Lord, and wept bitterly', vowing to dedicate her child to the Lord if he should answer her prayer. So it was that the boy Samuel grew up in the temple, and, while there, was called to be a prophet of God at a time when 'the word of the Lord was rare'. Not long after, Shiloh was destroyed, probably by the Philistines. Jeremiah takes this as an example of God's judgement on his people's wickedness.

Kiriath-jearim

"The Lord killed seventy of the men of Beth-shemesh because they looked into the Ark . . . 'Who is able to stand before Jehovah, this holy God?' they cried out. 'Where can we send the Ark from here?' So they sent messengers to the people at Kiriath-jearim and told them that the Philistines had brought back the Ark of the Lord. 'Come and get it!' they begged. So the men of Kiriath-jearim came and took the Ark to the hillside home of Abinadab; and installed his son Eleazar to be in charge of it. The Ark remained there for twenty years, and during that time all Israel was in sorrow because the Lord had seemingly abandoned them."
1 Samuel 6:19-7:2

The ark was the symbol of God's presence. Captured by the Philistines, and then returned, it began its slow journey to its final resting-place in Jerusalem. A sharp reminder that God's presence is utterly holy and not to be treated casually made the men of Beth-shemesh ask the nearby town of Kiriath-jearim to take over the responsibility for it. From Kiriath-jearim the ark was eventually taken to Jerusalem by David, with great rejoicing. The village of Abu Gosh stands on the site today. The hills above the village gave pilgrims travelling from the coast their first sight of the holy city of Jerusalem. It became customary for Jewish pilgrims to rend their clothes there to express their sorrow at the destruction of Jerusalem and its Temple.

Gibeah

"Then Samuel said to all the people, 'This is the man the Lord has chosen as your king. There isn't his equal in all of Israel!' And all the people shouted, 'Long live the king!' Then Samuel told the people again what the rights and duties of a king were; he wrote them in a book and put it in a special place before the Lord. Then Samuel sent the people home again. When Saul returned to his home at Gibe-ah, a band of men whose hearts the Lord had touched became his constant companions."
1 Samuel 10:24-26

Gibeah was the fortress and royal residence of Saul, as well as his home-town. It lies some three miles north of Jerusalem. On the same site King Hussein of Jordan started to build a palace, only to be overtaken by the events of the Six Day War in 1967. Excavations by W. F. Albright in 1922 brought to light a fortress, burnt near the end of the twelfth century BC, which may have been the scene of the crime described in Judges 19-20. A second level representing Saul's time included a two-storey fortress whose ground-floor storeroom contained pottery vessels of a certain simple luxury.

Ein Gedi

"After Saul's return from his battle with the Philistines, he was told that David had gone into the wilderness of Engedi; so he took three thousand special troops and went to search for him among the rocks and wild goats of the desert . . . After Saul had left the cave and gone on his way, David came out and shouted after him, 'My lord the king!' And when Saul looked around, David bowed low before him. Then he shouted to Saul, 'Why do you listen to the people who say that I am trying to harm you? This very day you have seen that it isn't true. The Lord placed you at my mercy back there in the cave and some of my men told me to kill you, but I spared you. For I said, "I will never harm him — he is the Lord's chosen king." . . .'"
1 Samuel 24:1, 2, 8-10

On the west shore of the Dead Sea is a sudden burst of greenery. The fresh-water stream at Ein Gedi flows down a gorge towards the shore, making possible a patch of sub-tropical cultivation which contrasts vividly with the desert around. The area abounds in caves, ideal hide-outs for a hunted man. David, on the run from Saul, would have had no difficulty in escaping, even from 3,000 men. He would have had no difficulty, either, in finding ready imagery for his psalms. The fresh stream in the desert surroundings, the mountains, the shadow of a mighty rock, the water cascading down cataracts and waterfalls, the gazelles and wild goats, all presented vivid pictures for his poetry.

The death of Saul

*"The Philistines had begun the battle
against Israel, and the Israelis fled
from them and were slaughtered whole-
sale on Mount Gilboa. The Philistines
closed in on Saul, and killed his sons
Jonathan, Abinidab, and Malchishua.
Then the archers overtook Saul and
wounded him badly. He groaned to his
armor bearer, 'Kill me with your
sword before these heathen Philistines
capture me and torture me.' But
his armor bearer was afraid to, so
Saul took his own sword and fell upon
the point of the blade . . . The next day
when the Philistines went out to strip
the dead, they found the bodies of Saul
and his three sons on Mount Gilboa.
They cut off Saul's head and stripped off
his armor and sent the wonderful news
of Saul's death to their idols and to the
people throughout their land. His armor
was placed in the temple of Ashtaroth,
and his body was fastened to the wall of
Beth-shan."*
1 Samuel 31:1-4, 8-10

The long, bitter struggle with the
Philistines led ultimately to tragedy: Saul
and Jonathan were slain on Mount Gilboa.
This view from the ancient city of
Beth-shan looks towards Gilboa in the
distance. Among the important finds were
two temples which may have been those
dedicated to Dagon and Ashtaroth in
which Saul's armour was displayed.
David's lament over Saul and Jonathan
in 2 Samuel 1 recalls their death more
personally and acutely: 'How are the
mighty fallen in the midst of battle! . . .'

Hebron

"Then representatives of all the tribes of Israel came to David at Hebron and gave him their pledge of loyalty. 'We are your blood brothers,' they said. 'And even when Saul was our king you were our real leader. The Lord has said that you should be the shepherd and leader of his people.' So David made a contract before the Lord with the leaders of Israel there at Hebron, and they crowned him king of Israel."
2 Samuel 5:1-3

Hebron had been the home of Abraham (see page 20). The highest town in Israel, it was now to be David's capital for seven and a half years until at last Jerusalem was taken. Later in David's reign, it was in Hebron that Absalom plotted his conspiracy against him.

Jerusalem

"David now led his troops to Jerusalem to fight against the Jebusites who lived there . . . So David made the stronghold of Zion (also called the City of David) his headquarters. Then, beginning at the old Millo section of the city, he built northward toward the present city center. So David became greater and greater, for the Lord God of heaven was with him."
2 Samuel 5:6, 9, 10

Looking up towards what was later to be the temple area, the view of Jerusalem from the south shows the part which was the ancient city of David. The domes above it are now those of mosques. Mount Zion may have been the whole area; today the name is given specifically to the hill on the left side of the picture (see too page 117). On the right the ground slopes away steeply to the Kidron Valley.

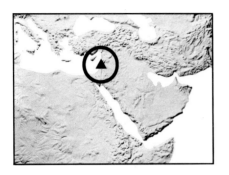

Tyre

"King Hiram of Tyre had always been a great admirer of David, so when he learned that David's son Solomon was the new king of Israel, he sent ambassadors to extend congratulations and good wishes. Solomon replied with a proposal about the Temple of the Lord he wanted to build. His father David, Solomon pointed out to Hiram, had not been able to build it because of the numerous wars going on, and he had been waiting for the Lord to give him peace. 'But now,' Solomon said to Hiram, 'the Lord my God has given Israel peace on every side; I have no foreign enemies or internal rebellions. So I am planning to build a Temple for the Lord my God, just as he instructed my father that I should do. For the Lord told him, "Your son, whom I will place upon your throne, shall build me a Temple." Now please assist me with this project. Send your woodsmen to the mountains of Lebanon to cut cedar timber for me, and I will send my men to work beside them, and I will pay your men whatever wages you ask; for as you know, no one in Israel can cut timber like you Sidonians!' " 1 Kings 5:1-6

Hiram, King of Tyre, had already supplied David with timber. Now at last David's son Solomon was to do what David had longed to do himself, build a 'house of the Lord'. The alliance with Tyre was a useful one. Solomon not only received cedar and cypress wood and gold. He was also given the services of a man to do all the bronze-casting for the new temple. In return, Hiram was given oil and wheat, also 'twenty cities in the land of Galilee' with which he was not particularly pleased. Tyre was at the height of its power, overshadowing its neighbour and rival, Sidon. Both towns had grown as a result of Phoenician sea-power. Originally an island, Tyre was linked to the land by a causeway at this time.

Solomon's Temple

"It was in the spring of the fourth year of Solomon's reign that he began the actual construction of the Temple. (This was 480 years after the people of Israel left their slavery in Egypt.) The Temple was ninety feet long, thirty feet wide, and forty-five feet high. All along the front of the Temple was a porch thirty feet long and fifteen feet deep."
1 Kings 6:1-3

The enormous temple area dominates the old city of Jerusalem. The rocky top of Mount Moriah on which it was built is now incorporated in the Mosque of Omar (see picture, page 27). The wall pictured here is at the highest, south-eastern end. The recently uncovered masonry on the right may go back to the time of Jehoshaphat of Judah/Ahab of Israel. Since Solomon's time, successive generations have added, rebuilt, destroyed and built again on the site, until now the area incorporates building from Crusader, Muslim, Roman and Herodian days and further back still.

Solomon's quarries

"The stones used in the construction of the Temple were prefinished at the quarry, so the entire structure was built without the sound of hammer, axe, or any other tool at the building site."
1 Kings 6:7

Why was this curious note included in the narrative? Deep below the old city of Jerusalem, a great cavern extends over 200 yards into the rock. The marks of the picks used to quarry out the rock can still be seen. Though so near to the Temple, no sound of the underground quarrying could carry to the actual construction site above.

Solomon's wide interests

"God gave Solomon great wisdom and understanding, and a mind with broad interests . . . He was a great naturalist, with interest in animals, birds, snakes, fish, and trees — from the great cedars of Lebanon down to the tiny hyssop which grows in cracks in the wall . . . King Solomon had a shipyard in Ezion-geber near Eloth on the Red Sea in the land of Edom, where he built a fleet of ships . . . Each year Solomon received gold worth about $20,000,000, besides sales taxes and profits from trade . . . Great men from many lands came to interview him and listen to his God-given wisdom. They brought him annual tribute . . ."
1 Kings 4:29, 33; 9:26; 10:14, 24, 25

Solomon was a man of many talents and wide interests. At Timna', near his port of Ezion-geber on the Red Sea, Solomon's copper-mines have been discovered. In a small valley, surrounded by the rocky hills of the Negev, the mines are being worked again today. On the top of the hill overlooking the site stood a watch-tower from which the king's men kept guard over those forced to labour in the copper-smelting pits, of which the remains can still be seen next to heaps of black slag.

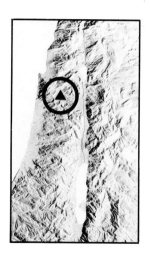

The cities of Solomon

"Solomon had conscripted forced labor to build the Temple, his palace, Fort Millo, the wall of Jerusalem, and the cities of Hazor, Megiddo, and Gezer . . . He also built cities for grain storage, cities in which to keep his chariots, cities for homes for his cavalry and chariot drivers, and resort cities . . . Solomon didn't conscript any Israelis for this work, although they became soldiers, officials, army officers, chariot commanders, and cavalrymen."
1 Kings 9:15, 19, 22

With his labour-force of captives Solomon's building programme was a vigorous one. This stairway at Megiddo leads to a gateway. Those at Hazor and Gezer are built to an identical plan: striking confirmation of the accuracy of the Bible text. Built to guard the pass through the Carmel range on the main north-south coastal highway, Megiddo reflects layer after layer of Bible history (see too pages 57 and 100). Here King Josiah was killed attempting to halt Egyptian forces on their way to aid crumbling Assyria. By New Testament times, Megiddo had seen so many battles that the writer of Revelation could use its name 'Armageddon' (or 'Har-Mageddon', the Hill of Megiddo) as a symbol of war.

Contest on Carmel

"So Ahab summoned all the people and the prophets to Mount Carmel. Then Elijah talked to them. 'How long are you going to waver between two opinions?' he asked the people. 'If the Lord is God, follow him! But if Baal is God, then follow him!'"
1 Kings 18:20, 21

A steep path leads down from the heights of Mount Carmel at its eastern end. Partway down is a natural amphitheatre. The track goes on down to the stream at the bottom. At the top of the path there is a view of the sea in one direction, the Valley of Jezreel and Galilee in the other. Rocks litter the natural theatre. Whether or not this was the exact site of Elijah's confrontation with the prophets of Baal, the conditions are right. Baal was supposed to control the elements, the rain and wind and fire. But God showed himself supreme 'When all the people saw it, they fell on their faces; and they said, "The Lord, he is God; the Lord, he is God."'

Jezreel

"Naboth, a man from Jezreel, had a vineyard on the outskirts of the city near King Ahab's palace. One day the king talked to him about selling him his land. 'I want it for a garden,' the king explained, 'because it's so convenient to the palace.' . . . But Naboth replied, 'Not on your life! That land has been in my family for generations.'"
1 Kings 21:1-3

It was Ahab's wife Jezebel who then took matters into her own hands. Naboth was quoting the law which protected the people from just such arbitrary acts of despotism and land-grabbing. But Jezebel cared nothing for the law; it took Elijah's words to reduce Ahab to repentance — and God's judgement to put an end to Jezebel's evil influence.

Ahab's palace

"Just as the sun was going down the cry ran through his troops. 'It's all over — return home! The king is dead!' And his body was taken to Samaria and buried there. When his chariot and armor were washed beside the pool of Samaria, where the prostitutes bathed, dogs came and licked the king's blood just as the Lord had said would happen. The rest of Ahab's history — including the story of the ivory palace and the cities he built — is written in The Annals of the Kings of Israel.*"*
1 Kings 22:37-39

The magnificent hill-top city of Samaria was built by Omri and made his capital. Ahab erected a temple to Baal there, and then built a luxurious palace. More than 200 pieces of ivory were discovered in a store-room, during the excavation of the site. This picture shows the remains of the palace itself, high up on the hill among ruins from the time of the Roman occupation, centuries later. A 10-yard-long pool, probably the one in which Ahab's blood-stained chariot was washed down, has also been uncovered. The prophet Amos, about a hundred years later, tells of people who 'feel secure on the mountain of Samaria . . . who lie upon beds of ivory', and goes on to depict their downfall.

The chariot cities

"King Ben-hadad of Syria now mobilized his army and, with thirty-two allied nations and their hordes of chariots and horses, besieged Samaria, the Israeli capital. He sent this message into the city to King Ahab of Israel: 'Your silver and gold are mine, as are your prettiest wives and the best of your children!' "
1 Kings 20:1-3

The threat of Ben-hadad, for all his bravado, was fought off, both in the hills and later on the plain. Chariots featured, too, in Ahab's battle with Shalmaneser III at Qarqar: according to Shalmaneser Ahab had a force of 2,000 chariots. The picture shows the remains of the stables for his horses at Megiddo. The water-troughs and hitching-posts, also from Megiddo, are shown erected in the picture below, taken at the Rockefeller Museum, Jerusalem. Solomon had established Megiddo, Hazor and Gezer as chariot-cities: 'he had fourteen hundred chariots and twelve thousand horsemen, whom he stationed in the chariot cities and with the king in Jerusalem' (1 Kings 10: 26)

The siege of Samaria

"Now the land of Israel was filled with Assyrian troops for three years besieging Samaria, the capital city of Israel. Finally, in the ninth year of King Hoshea's reign, Samaria fell and the people of Israel were exiled to Assyria . . . This disaster came upon the nation of Israel because the people worshiped other gods, thus sinning against the Lord their God who had brought them safely out of their slavery in Egypt. They had followed the evil customs of the nations which the Lord had cast out before them. The people of Israel had also secretly done many things that were wrong . . ."
2 Kings 17:5-9

The prophets had warned the people of the coming invasion, warned them to turn from their sin and from the judgement to come. The threat from Assyria, for so long just over the horizon, became an ugly reality. The crumbling walls on the heights of Samaria look down over a scene which, in 722 BC, saw the culmination of three years of siege. The city fell. The people were deported. The area was repopulated by Assyria with other conquered peoples. These inter-married with the few Israelites who were left, forming the Samaritan people so despised and hated in the time of Jesus, and surviving today as a few hundred people with their own traditions and worship.

Lachish

"During the fourteenth year of the reign of King Hezekiah, King Sennacherib of Assyria besieged and captured all the fortified cities of Judah. King Hezekiah sued for peace and sent this message to the king of Assyria at Lachish: 'I have done wrong. I will pay whatever tribute you demand if you will only go away.' The king of Assyria then demanded a settlement of $1,500,000. To gather this amount, King Hezekiah used all the silver stored in the Temple and in the palace treasury."
2 Kings 18:13-15

Eight years after the fall of Samaria and the exile of the northern kingdom of Israel, the Assyrians attack Judah to the south. Lachish, a fortified city in the foot-hills of Judah in the approaches to Jerusalem, had first to be immobilized before the capital itself. The 'tell', or mound of Lachish, can be seen in the distance in the picture. The smaller picture shows the remains on top of the mound. Joshua had taken Lachish in an attack lasting two days: signs of burning from that time can still be seen. The fortifications were strengthened under Rehoboam. The siege by the Assyrian general Sennacherib was vividly portrayed in reliefs on the walls of his palace at Nineveh (now in the British Museum). The heavy destruction was shown in the remains discovered by archaeologists — and by a mass grave holding 1,500 bodies. With Lachish wiped out and the line of support from Egypt thus cut off, Sennacherib marched on Jerusalem.

The defense of Jerusalem

"Then Isaiah said to Hezekiah, 'Listen to the word of the Lord: The time will come when everything in this palace shall be carried to Babylon. All the treasures of your ancestors will be taken — nothing shall be left . . .' The rest of the history of Hezekiah and his great deeds — including the pool and the conduit he made and how he brought water into the city — are recorded in The Annals of the Kings of Judah. *When he died, his son Manasseh became the new king."*
2 Kings 20:16-17, 20-21

As king of Judah, Hezekiah had initiated thorough and widespread reforms. He reopened the Temple and established its services, attacked pagan practices, undertook extensive rebuilding and the fortification of Jerusalem against the threat of invasion. One of his measures was to ensure that there was access inside the city walls to water from one of Jerusalem's principal water-supplies, the Gihon spring, pictured here. To do so he dug a tunnel 1,750 feet through solid rock from the spring to bring the water to a pool (the Pool of Siloam) inside the walls. The tunnel was discovered in 1880, including an inscription (now in the Istanbul Archaeological Museum) graphically recording the event. Hezekiah won a reprieve for Jerusalem: the city was not destroyed until the attack of Nebuchad-nezzar of Babylon in 587 BC.

Return to Jerusalem

"Three days after my arrival at Jerusalem I stole out during the night, taking only a few men with me; for I hadn't told a soul about the plans for Jerusalem which God had put into my heart . . . But now I told them, 'You know full well the tragedy of our city; it lies in ruins and the gates are burned. Let us rebuild the wall of Jerusalem and rid ourselves of this disgrace!' Then I told them about the desire God had put into my heart, and of my conversation with the king, and the plan to which he had agreed. They replied at once, 'Good! Let's rebuild the wall!'"
Nehemiah 2:11, 12, 17, 18

Nehemiah in exile was cupbearer to the king of Persia. In this influential position he was able to take action following reports he had heard of the state of Jerusalem. A man of prayer, he was also a man of great organizational ability. Despite opposition, under his leadership the people rebuilt the walls of Jerusalem in under two months. Nehemiah was appointed governor in 445 BC, went back to Persia for a time, and returned later to reform abuses that had arisen in his absence. With Ezra, he re-established worship and obedience to the law of God.

Most of the present walls of Jerusalem date from medieval times. Some of the massive masonry from Herod's Temple survives. This was started in 19 BC and finished only a few years before its destruction by the Romans in AD 70. This picture shows the 'Golden Gate', in the position of the one east-facing gate of Herod's Temple.

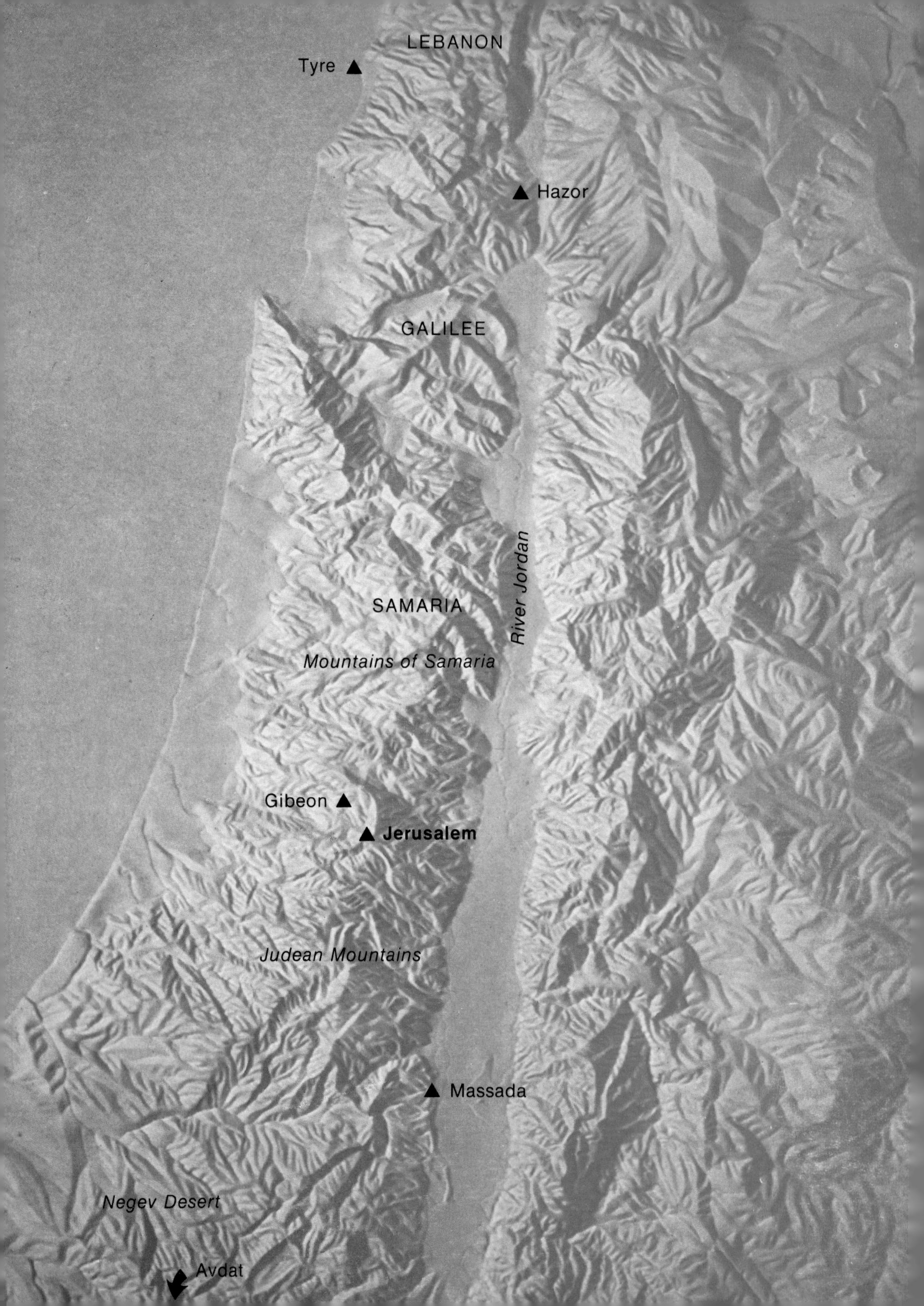

LEBANON

Tyre ▲

▲ Hazor

GALILEE

River Jordan

SAMARIA

Mountains of Samaria

Gibeon ▲

▲ **Jerusalem**

Judean Mountains

▲ Massada

Negev Desert

▲ Avdat

PART FOUR

Poets and Prophets

Job

"There lived in the land of Uz a man named Job—a good man who feared God and stayed away from evil. He had a large family of seven sons and three daughters, and was immensely wealthy, for he owned 7,000 sheep, 3,000 camels, 500 teams of oxen, 500 female donkeys, and employed many servants. He was, in fact, the richest cattleman in that entire area. Every year when each of Job's sons had a birthday, he invited his brothers and sisters to his home for a celebration. On these occasions they would eat and drink with great merriment. When these birthday parties ended —and sometimes they lasted several days—Job would summon his children to him and sanctify them, getting up early in the morning and offering a burnt offering for each of them. For Job said, 'Perhaps my sons have sinned and turned away from God in their hearts.' This was Job's regular practice."
Job 1:1-5

We do not know who wrote the book of Job, or when and where it was written. It is tempting to think it was the product of fireside storytelling, told and retold since the patriarchal times in which it was set. It may, however, have arisen out of the much more sophisticated environment that also produced Proverbs and Ecclesiastes, as an intellectual protest against the religious dogmatism and blinkered theology which reduced God to a set of rules. It may have seemed obvious that when Job lost his wealth and his ten children and was stricken with illness, it was God judging him for his sins. This is what his friends said. But that was not the answer . . .

The Lord is my shepherd

"Because the Lord is my Shepherd,
I have everything I need!
He lets me rest in the meadow grass
and leads me beside the quiet streams.
He restores my failing health. He helps
me do what honors him the most.
Even when walking through the dark
valley of death I will not be afraid, for
you are close beside me, guarding,
guiding all the way . . ."
Psalm 23:1-4

The Psalms were both the hymn-book
and anthology of poetry of Israel.
They include hymns for religious
occasions, such as the 'songs of
ascents', sung by the worshippers in
procession behind the ark at a festival.
Others had titles suggesting they were
for thanksgiving or lament or teaching.
Many are very personal, the expression
of trust, or despair, or joy, or wonder.
A picture of sheep grazing in lush
meadows beside still waters is not an
easy one to find in the lands of the
Middle East. It was an ideal, a beautiful
picture of peace and security. For the
one whose shepherd is God himself it can
be realized even in conditions which are
less than ideal — even among enemies
and facing the threat of danger and
death.

Gazelles on the mountains

"As the deer pants for water, so I long for you, O God. I thirst for God, the living God. Where can I find him to come and stand before him? Day and night I weep for his help, and all the while my enemies taunt me. 'Where is this God of yours?' they scoff."
Psalm 42:1-3

The Psalms are rich with imagery from the countryside and desert. These gazelles are in the gorge of Avdat, in the Negev desert in the south of Israel. Hart, or deer, are no longer to be found in Israel—the last disappeared early this century. In the desert it is only too easy to appreciate the aching longing for water expressed in the psalm, which the poet uses to picture his longing for renewed fellowship with God.

Mount Zion

"How great is the Lord! How much we should praise him. He lives upon Mount Zion in Jerusalem . . .
Go, inspect the city! Walk around and count her many towers! Note her walls and tour her palaces, so that you can tell your children.
For this great God is our God forever and ever."
Psalm 48:1, 12-14

Mount Zion was one of the hills of Jerusalem. Traditionally the name has been referred to the one pictured here; but David's City itself was further to the east, and it is clear that Zion included the religious centre of Israel, the Temple. So it can be generally equated with Jerusalem, the aspiration of every pilgrim, the stronghold of Israel, the symbol of the nation under God.

Massada, the fortress

"We live within the shadow of the Al-mighty, sheltered by the God who is above all gods. This I declare, that he alone is my refuge, my place of safety; he is my God, and I am trusting him . . . His faithful promises are your armor. Now you don't need to be afraid of the dark any more, nor fear the dangers of the day; nor dread the plagues of darkness, nor disasters in the morning."
Psalm 91:1-6

Just over two miles from the Dead Sea, in the rocky Wilderness of Judea, rises the great rock slab of Massada, or Metsuda, a fortress or stronghold. Here the Jews made their last heroic stand against the Romans in AD 73. After three years of siege, the defenders put themselves to death rather than fall into enemy hands. Several times in the Psalms David calls the Lord his fortress. It may have been to this place that he came when fleeing from Saul: 'David and his men went up to the stronghold.' In any case it was a powerful image of the fact that God would not only defend him but himself be his refuge and fortress. At Massada today can be seen storehouses, reservoirs and fortifications from the time of the Jewish Revolt; also remains of a palace built by Herod, and ruins of a Roman fort.

Wisdom in the streets

"Wisdom shouts in the streets for a hearing. She calls out to the crowds along Main Street, and to the judges in their courts, and to everyone in all the land: 'You simpletons!' she cries. 'How long will you go on being fools? How long will you scoff at wisdom and fight the facts? Come here and listen to me! . . .'"
Proverbs 1:20-23

The Old Testament 'wisdom literature' includes Proverbs, Job and Ecclesiastes. Job was written in the form of a great poetic drama. Proverbs is at the other literary extreme, consisting of a collection of short pithy thoughts. But the basic concern is the same: to seek out what is true in life. In Proverbs this is expressed in the form of 'wise sayings' expressing what is 'true in general', what is normally the case in ordinary, daily life. They are not so much promises from God as descriptions of life under God. Idleness, falsehood, dishonesty, crooked dealing, adultery are not the way to wisdom and life. Trusting in God, living a life that is consistent with the way he has been created, this is how man has been designed to live and so the way to true success and happiness.

An overgrown vineyard

*"I walked by the field of a certain lazy
fellow and saw that it was overgrown
with thorns, and covered with weeds;
and its walls were broken down. Then,
as I looked, I learned this lesson:
'A little extra sleep,
A little more slumber,
A little folding of the hands to rest'
means that poverty will break in upon
you suddenly like a robber, and violently
like a bandit."*
Proverbs 24:30-34

In graphic, humorous detail the point is
made. Laziness inevitably leads to ruin.
Again, this is what is usually the case; it
is a simple observation of life. The nations
around Israel at this time also had their
'wisdom books', such as the Egyptian
Wisdom of Amenemope. Some have con-
cluded that the Bible's wisdom is therefore no more than imitation. But the
whole point of wisdom literature was to
distil what is universally true. If this has
been well expressed by secular man, then
its truth can be underlined. But 'wisdom'
which does not relate human life to the
one who created and sustains it is not
truly wise; for the 'fear of the Lord is
the beginning of wisdom'.

Life under the sun

*"In my opinion, nothing is worthwhile;
everything is futile. For what does a man
get for all his hard work? Generations
come and go but it makes no difference.
The sun rises and sets and hurries
around to rise again . . . everything is
unutterably weary and tiresome."*
Ecclesiastes 1:2-9

Life without God is vain, empty, fruitless.
The seasons come and go, nothing
changes, nothing is new. In love or war,
toil or leisure, life goes on, life 'under the
sun' is apparently pointless, meaningless.
If all this has a twentieth-century ring to
it, it is not by accident. For 'the
Preacher' was doing what many twentieth-
century writers are also doing: expressing
the cynicism and meaninglessness of
man and the daily round. But Ecclesiastes
also introduces a wider perspective, that
of life under God—though he scarcely
begins to give the answers. As the Bible
makes plain, these await the coming of
the One who can make all things new.

Song of songs

" 'I am dark but beautiful, O girls of Jerusalem, tanned as the dark tents of Kedar . . . Don't look down on me, you city girls, just because my complexion is so dark—the sun has tanned me. My brothers were angry with me and sent me out into the sun to tend the vineyards, but see what it has done to me! Tell me, O one I love, where are you leading your flock today? Where will you be at noon? For I will come and join you there instead of wandering like a vagabond among the flocks of your companions.' "
The Song of Solomon 1:5-7

The Bible's collection of poetry and wisdom would be incomplete without the pure lyric feeling and joy in love expressed in the Song of Solomon. It is difficult to unravel the 'story' expressed in the dialogue between bridegroom and bride. Some see it as the tale of a beautiful country girl taken to the King's court, who is torn between the royal suitor and her rustic lover. But it may be that it is simply a collection of love-songs grouped together with little connection. What is clear is that the Bible contains in this book a celebration of the purity, beauty and wonder of human love. It was Greek philosophy that introduced the idea that physical love belongs to the lower nature, and that things of the soul have no connection with things of the body. The Bible sees no such division. The God who created man to love him also created man and woman and their love for one another.

Crimson dye

"Come, let's talk this over! says the Lord; no matter how deep the stain of your sins, I can take it out and make you as clean as freshly fallen snow. Even if you are stained as red as crimson, I can make you white as wool!" Isaiah 1:18

After Solomon's death, the unity and wealth of the kingdom was disrupted by civil war and the division of the kingdom into north and south, Judah and Israel. By Isaiah's time, Judah under King Uzziah (who reigned about 790-740 BC) was again prosperous. The danger was not civil war or even invasion but the sins of luxury and self-indulgence. Whatever the danger and whatever the sin, Isaiah remained faithful to his prophetic message, recalling men from evil and promising God's forgiveness in response to repentance and faith.

Tyre and Sidon

"Weep, O ships of Tyre, returning home from distant lands! Weep for your harbor, for it is gone! . . . Be ashamed, O Sidon . . ." Isaiah 23:1, 4

The Phoenicians of Tyre and Sidon were indeed the merchants and seafarers of the nations. Isaiah's prophecy about Sidon (pictured here) came about when the Assyrians under Sennacherib marched on the city and defeated it. Much of Isaiah's book is concerned with the nations around, both inveighing against their immorality and warning of the dangers of invasion or alliance. Because of their strategic importance in commerce and communications, Sidon and Tyre (pictured on page 84) continued to be dominated by foreign powers, down to Roman times. It was here that Jesus healed the daughter of the Syro-Phoenician woman, and many listened to his teaching there.

131

Water in the desert

"When the poor and needy seek water and there is none and their tongues are parched from thirst, then I will answer when they cry to me. I, Israel's God, will not ever forsake them. I will open rivers for them on high plateaus! I will give them fountains of water in the valleys! In the deserts will be pools of water, and rivers fed by springs shall flow across the dry, parched ground . . . Everyone will see this miracle and understand that it is God who did it, Israel's Holy One."
Isaiah 41:17, 18, 20

From political intrigue and the threat of invasion, from the horrors of war and exile, Isaiah called the people to lift up their eyes to a future in which God would wipe away their tears, the land would be restored to them and God would dwell in harmony with his people. In a country with such a large proportion of barren desert, it was natural for the symbol of this messianic rule to become 'the desert that blossomed'.

Gehenna

"The people of Judah have sinned before my very eyes, says the Lord. They have set up their idols right in my own Temple, polluting it. They have built the altar called Topheth in the Valley of Ben-Hinnom, and there they burn to death their little sons and daughters as sacrifices to their gods — a deed so horrible I've never even thought of it, let alone commanded it to be done. The time is coming, says the Lord, when that valley's name will be changed from 'Topheth,' or the 'Valley of Ben-Hinnom,' to the 'Valley of Slaughter';
. . . I will end the happy singing and laughter in the streets of Jerusalem and in the cities of Judah, and the joyous voices of the bridegrooms and brides. For the land shall lie in desolation."
Jeremiah 7:30-32, 34

Jeremiah is generally associated with gloom and disaster: but as a sensitive and gentle man this was the last sort of message that he wanted to bring. It is a measure of his utter faithfulness that he stuck to his calling regardless of personal misfortune. The Valley of Hinnom, pictured here, curves round the south-western side of the city of Jerusalem. In Jeremiah's time it was associated with the evils of child-sacrifice. It was also to become the city rubbish-dump, where the refuse was continually burning. The name Hinnom, or Gehenna, became a symbol of hell itself.

The potter

"Here is another message to Jeremiah from the Lord. Go down to the shop where clay pots and jars are made and I will talk to you there. I did as he told me, and found the potter working at his wheel. But the jar that he was forming didn't turn out as he wished, so he kneaded it into a lump and started again. Then the Lord said: O Israel, can't I do to you as this potter has done to his clay?"
Jeremiah 18:1-6

As the lump of clay is turned on the wheel, it is formed by the potter's hand into a jar or bowl. This was a vivid picture of the way God 'moulds' his people, and one that recurs in the Bible. Equally, as here, the pot that did not shape up as intended could be scrapped and started again. 'Behold, like the clay in the potter's hand, so are you in my hand, O house of Israel.'

A basket of figs

"After Nebuchadnezzar, king of Babylon, had captured and enslaved Jeconiah (son of Jehoiakim), king of Judah, and exiled him to Babylon along with the princes of Judah and the skilled tradesmen — the carpenters and blacksmiths — the Lord gave me this vision. I saw two baskets of figs placed in front of the Temple in Jerusalem. In one basket there were fresh, just-ripened figs, but in the other the figs were spoiled and moldy — too rotten to eat. Then the Lord said to me, 'What do you see, Jeremiah?' I replied, 'Figs, some very good and some very bad.'"
Jeremiah 24:1-3

Many of the prophecies were delivered in striking pictorial terms. (Ezekiel in exile even built models under the fascinated gaze of his watchers.) Nebuchadrezzar had put on the throne of Judah a puppet-king, Zedekiah — the Old Testament account of this is supported by the Babylonian Chronicle. The new king banished the previous leaders of the nation and surrounded himself with poor substitutes — Jeremiah's 'good and bad figs'. The prophet risked his neck for his outspokenness: God would renew his covenant with his faithful, exiled people, but Zedekiah and his princes would be utterly destroyed.

The pool at Gibeon

"In October, Ishmael . . . arrived in Mizpah, accompanied by ten men. Gedaliah invited them to dinner. While they were eating, Ishmael and the ten men in league with him suddenly jumped up, pulled out their swords and killed Gedaliah . . . But when Johanan (son of Kareah) and the rest of the guerrilla leaders heard what Ishmael had done, they took all their men and set out to stop him. They caught up with him at the pool near Gibeon."
Jeremiah 41:1, 2, 11, 12

Excavations at a site about 6 miles north of Jerusalem revealed a large pit with stairs leading down to a tunnel. The tunnel leads to a well outside the walls of the city. In the pit were jars inscribed with the name of the city: Gibeon. The events of the 'great pool of Gibeon' were part of the tangled aftermath of the Babylonian invasion, the murder of the governor Gedaliah being followed by the counter-attack and eventual flight to Egypt — Jeremiah being unwillingly taken along with the rest.

The Wailing Wall

"Jerusalem's streets, once thronged with people, are silent how. Like a widow broken with grief, she sits alone in her mourning. She, once queen of nations, is now a slave . . . O Lord, forever you remain the same! Your throne continues from generation to generation. Why do you forget us forever? Why do you forsake us for so long? Turn us around and bring us back to you again! That is our only hope! Give us back the joys we used to have! Or have you utterly rejected us? Are you angry with us still?" Lamentations 1:1, 5:19-22

The beginning and end of Lamentations sum up the aspirations of a people denied their spiritual home: 'How long, O Lord . . .' The Wailing Wall, or Western Wall of the former Temple in Jerusalem, has been the focus of the sorrow and hope of the dispersed people of Israel down to the present day. Since Israel's repossession of the wall it has become a shrine and symbol of national renewal.

The cedar tree

" 'The Lord God says: I, myself, will take the finest and most tender twig from the top of the highest cedar, and I, myself, will plant it on the top of Israel's highest mountain. It shall become a noble cedar, bringing forth branches and bearing fruit. Animals of every sort will gather under it; its branches will shelter every kind of bird. And everyone shall know that it is I, the Lord, who cuts down the high trees and exalts the low, that I make the green tree wither and the dry tree grow. I, the Lord, have said that I would do it, and I will.' "
Ezekiel 17:22-24

Ezekiel, deported to Babylon, was called to be a prophet when he was thirty — the age at which, under normal circumstances, he would have been received into the priesthood. With emotional intensity and vivid symbolism he expressed the concern and longing of an exile for his land and the nation's spiritual renewal. On the day that Jerusalem fell, Ezekiel's wife died, summing up the complete personal identification of the prophet with the subject of his message. His oracle about the cedar of Lebanon and the eagle which took a branch from its top is typical of his soaring prophetic imagination. Today the magnificent cedars of Lebanon, once the source of timber for Solomon's Temple, are reduced to a few isolated groves of trees high in the mountains.

The watchman

*"I have appointed you as a watchman
for the people of Israel; therefore listen
to what I say and warn them for me.
When I say to the wicked, 'O wicked
man, you will die!' and you don't tell
him what I say, so that he does not
repent—that wicked person will die in
his sins, but I will hold you responsible
for his death. But if you warn him to
repent and he doesn't, he will die in his
sin, and you will not be responsible."*
Ezekiel 33:7-9

Small towers from which watchmen can
keep guard over valuable crops and olive-
groves are a familiar sight among the
hills of Judah and Samaria. With char-
acteristic concern, Ezekiel sees his role
as a matter of life and death. If as
watchman he fails to warn the people of
their impending fate, their blood would
be on his head. Such earnestness and
utter dedication was typical of the
'prophets of the Lord'; theirs was a key
role, carrying heavy responsibility both
to God and to his people.

O Israel, return

"O Israel, return to the Lord, your God, for you have been crushed by your sins . . . Then I will cure you of idolatry and faithlessness, and my love will know no bounds, for my anger will be forever gone! I will refresh Israel like the dew from heaven; she will blossom as the lily and root deeply in the soil like cedars in Lebanon. Her branches will spread out, as beautiful as olive trees, fragrant as the forests of Lebanon. Her people will return from exile far away and rest beneath my shadow. They will be a watered garden and blossom like grapes and be as fragrant as the wines of Lebanon."
Hosea 14:1, 4-7

Hosea was another prophet deeply iden- tified with his message. As a northerner, he loved the land and its gentle land-- scapes, like this peaceful scene in Galilee. He also loved his wife, and it was her unfaithfulness which showed him how agonizing it was to God that his people should be unfaithful and rebellious. He shows God's love for his people, his long- ing to forgive them, his longing to restore them to the peace and content expressed in the picture of lily and poplar, olive and vine.

The ploughman

" 'The time will come when there will be such abundance of crops, that the harvest time will scarcely end before the farmer starts again to sow another crop, and the terraces of grapes upon the hills of Israel will drip sweet wine! I will restore the fortunes of my people Israel, and they shall rebuild their ruined cities, and live in them again, and they shall plant vineyards and gardens and eat their crops and drink their wine. I will firmly plant them there upon the land that I have given them; they shall not be pulled up again,' says the Lord your God."
Amos 9:13-15

Amos was a countryman sickened by the corruption, immorality and social inequality of Samaria, capital city of Israel. In calling the people to repentance and righteousness he was unpopular and ignored. Only in these last verses of his prophecy does he allow a hope for the future to shine through. In rural areas of the Middle East today a wooden plough is still used, drawn by a horse or by oxen.

A pagan shrine

"At that same time, says the Lord. . . . I
will put an end to all witchcraft—there
will be no more fortune-tellers to
consult—and destroy all your idols.
Never again will you worship what you
have made, and I will abolish the heathen
shrines from among you, and destroy
the cities where your idol temples
stand . . . 'How can we make up to you
for what we've done?' you ask. 'Shall
we bow before the Lord with offerings
of yearling calves?' . . . No, he has told
you what he wants, and this is all it is:
to be fair and just and merciful, and to
walk humbly with your God."
Micah 5:10, 12-14; 6:6, 8

The prophets combined demands for
social justice with denunciation of the
evils of pagan religion. For immorality
fed on paganism, wanton disregard for
human values on a religion which had
no moral concern. This altar at Byblos,
Lebanon was dedicated to pagan practices
going back to Canaanite times.

The storehouse

" 'Will a man rob God? Surely not! And yet you have robbed me,' 'What do you mean? When did we ever rob you?' 'You have robbed me of the tithes and offerings due to me. And so the awesome curse of God is cursing you, for your whole nation has been robbing me. Bring all the tithes into the storehouse so that there will be food enough in my Temple; if you do, I will open up the windows of heaven for you and pour out a blessing so great you won't have room enough to take it in! Try it! Let me prove it to you! Your crops will be large, for I will guard them from insects and plagues. Your grapes won't shrivel away before they ripen,' says the Lord of Hosts. 'And all nations will call you blessed, for you will be a land sparkling with happiness. These are the promises of the Lord of Hosts.' "
Malachi 3:8-12

The pillars of a building at Hazor, in northern Galilee, are thought to have belonged to a storehouse. A rural economy depended to a large extent on storage of oil and grain, and the storehouse to Malachi was a test of the people's devotion to God. Then, as now, it was a question of whether the people would show where their heart was by putting their money there also. Throughout Old Testament times, the choice was simple, but difficult. Will man love God with all his heart and soul and all he is, following the ways of his law and his creation? Or will he go his own way, with all the disastrous results recorded in Old Testament history? Today the choice is as acutely necessary as ever.